This journal belongs to

....

© 2013 by Barbour Publishing, Inc.

ISBN 978-1-63609-082-5

All rights reserved. No part of this publication may be reproduced or transmitted for commercial purposes, except for brief quotations in printed reviews, without written permission of the publisher. Reproduced text may not be used on the World Wide Web.

Churches and other noncommercial interests may reproduce portions of this book without the express written permission of Barbour Publishing, provided that the text does not exceed 500 words or 5 percent of the entire book, whichever is less, and that the text is not material quoted from another publisher. When reproducing text from this book, include the following credit line: "From *My Prayer Journal: His Praise Is on My Lips*, published by Barbour Publishing, Inc. Used by permission."

Scripture quotations marked AMPC are taken from the Amplified® Bible, Classic Edition, Copyright © 1954, 1958, 1962, 1964, 1987 by The Lockman Foundation. Used by permission.

Scripture quotations marked PHILLIPS are taken from J. B. Phillips, "The New Testament in Modern English", 1962 edition, published by HarperCollins. Used by permission. All rights reserved.

Scripture quotations marked KJV are taken from the King James Version of the Bible.

Scripture quotations marked NIV are taken from the HOLY BIBLE, NEW INTERNATIONAL VERSION®. NIV®. Copyright © 1973, 1978, 1984, 2011 by Biblica, Inc.™ Used by permission. All rights reserved worldwide.

Scripture quotations marked NKJV are taken from the New King James Version®. Copyright © 1982 by Thomas Nelson, Inc. Used by permission. All rights reserved.

Scripture quotations marked NLT are taken from the *Holy Bible*. New Living Translation copyright© 1996, 2004, 2015 by Tyndale House Foundation. Used by permission of Tyndale House Publishers, Inc. Carol Stream, Illinois 60188. All rights reserved.

Published by Barbour Publishing, Inc., 1810 Barbour Drive, Uhrichsville, Ohio 44683, www.barbourbooks.com

Our mission is to inspire the world with the life-changing message of the Bible.

 Member of the
Evangelical Christian
Publishers Association

Printed in China.

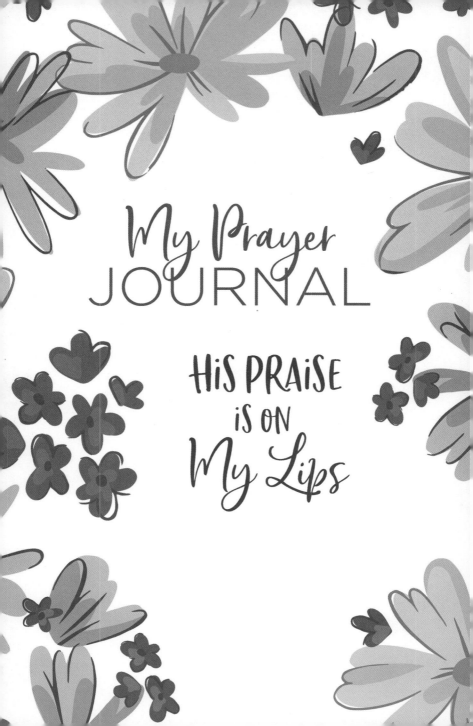

My Prayer
JOURNAL

HiS PRAiSE
iS ON
My Lips

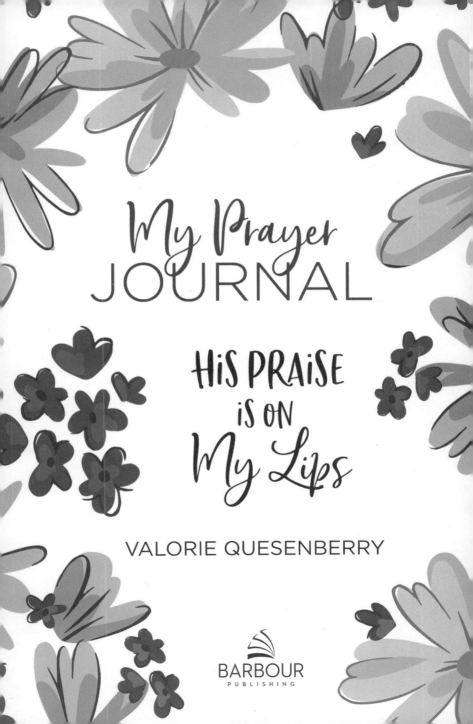

My Prayer
JOURNAL

HiS PRAiSE
iS ON
My Lips

VALORIE QUESENBERRY

BARBOUR
PUBLISHING

Let everything that breathes sing
praises to the LORD! Praise the LORD!
PSALM 150:6 NLT

The language of praise is one we need to speak fluently. As women, we are able to appreciate the nuances in the world around us, and this sensitivity can make us more aware of God's greatness and His work in our lives.

Calvary provides the basis for our worship, but it doesn't stop there. From the wonders of nature to simple daily blessings, there are countless reasons for praise.

In our professions, marriages, and homes, in our spiritual lives, alone or in a crowd, today and tomorrow, we can join in the celebration with His praise on our lips.

We can never know who or what we are till we know at least something of what God is.

A. W. TOZER

Praise for
THE GOD OF
SPLENDOR

THE ORIGINAL FATHER

*"I will be a father to you, and you shall be my sons
and daughters, says the Lord Almighty."*
2 CORINTHIANS 6:18 PHILLIPS

Fatherhood is a hot topic. Everyone has an opinion on dads—good or bad. And everyone has a father—present or not, engaged or not, loving or not. The recent rise in father absenteeism has come with a hefty price: Fatherlessness contributes to almost every social ill, from substance abuse to violent crime.

Now there is a growing awareness of the vital role fathers play in the lives of their kids. There is even a National Fatherhood Initiative dedicated to informing the public about the importance of fathers and offering encouragement and suggestions for busy dads.

Christians have always believed in the mission of fathers because they know the One who set the earthly pattern—the heavenly Father. As children in the family of God, believers experience the love, strength, provision, and protection that He gives.

Psychologists have said that those who were neglected or abused by their earthly fathers find it difficult to accept God as a Father. For them, we must declare that He is the original—the One who made the pattern and the only One who fills the role perfectly. For everyone who longs to know what a Father really is, He waits in welcome, and there is none that can compare to Him.

*Father in heaven, thank You for being the
example of perfect Fatherhood. Amen.*

THE FORTRESS

*The L*ORD *is my rock, and my fortress, and my
deliverer; my God, my strength, in whom I will trust.*
PSALM 18:2 KJV

A fortress boasts of protection. To inhabit a fortress is to live in safety. Yet, earthly strongholds have weaknesses. Medieval castles could not always keep out the marauding invaders because moats and drawbridges and turrets can only stall progress for so long. Neither could forts in the early American wilderness hold back the enemy since fiery arrows make quick work of wooden planks. Even the fortress of Masada, whose brave defenders held against unbelievable odds, could not last indefinitely against the catapults and ramparts and battering rams of the Tenth Roman Legion. All human strongholds will ultimately collapse.

But God will not. He is "a mighty Fortress" as Martin Luther penned. He is the citadel, the impenetrable tower of strength for all who run to Him. Millions have found refuge in Him, and there is room still for more.

Every woman needs a fortress because assaults will come—a child's illness, a husband's job crisis, a family disaster, a friend's diagnosis, a wrecked future. When the earthly walls begin to crumple and fall, God is a source of strength. Whatever the landscape of life, whatever ill winds blow across the soul, He is forever the mighty Fortress.

*God, I praise You for the strength
You give to me. Amen.*

THE GOD WHO SACRIFICES

Christ also has loved us and given
Himself for us, an offering and a sacrifice
to God for a sweet-smelling aroma.
EPHESIANS 5:2 NKJV

There was once a place called the Valley of Hinnom where the Canaanites worshipped their god Molech. This god demanded sacrifice—vegetables, cattle, and humans. The large idol was made of brass or bronze with a hollow space inside where a fire burned. The hands were outstretched and very hot. Small children were placed in the hands of the statue and burned alive as a sacrifice; some accounts say the hands were slanted, allowing the child to actually roll down into the flames. God specifically forbade the Israelites from entering into this pagan practice (Leviticus 18:21).

Many pagan religions demand sacrifice of some kind, an act of service or humility to appease the god. Some worshippers make pilgrimages, endure self-inflicted pain, pay money, and even engage in warfare as tribute to their god.

Followers of Christ are the only worshippers whose God sacrificed for them. He didn't demand we do anything; He did it all. He gave His Son to be sacrificed for our sins on a cross outside Jerusalem. Jesus brings us to the Father, and there is mercy for all who call on Him because He paid the price.

God, I worship You because You
sacrificed Your Son for me. Amen.

MANNA MAKER

And Moses said unto them, This is the bread
which the LORD hath given you to eat.
EXODUS 16:15 KJV

Imagine a barren place of sand, heat, and scrub brush. See thousands of tents spread out across the landscape. Hear the voices of hungry children. Listen to weary men address the leader in frustration. There are no markets, no gardens, and no root cellars. There is no way for these families to provide food for themselves. They are stranded and doomed to starve.

At least, that's what they think. God has a miracle on the edge of heaven. He is about to send them more food than they could possibly eat. And He'll do it not just once, but until they are settled in the Promised Land.

Life brings bleak places to everyone, and Christians are not protected from hard times. But God is the Manna Maker. He provides for those who follow Him. For the Hebrews who were prone to doubt and complain, He was faithful. And He is still the same today. His generous and good hand is at work. Whatever is needed—food, clothing, a car, funds for an unpaid bill—He has the resources to provide. The Israelites had never seen this type of bread before, and you and I may not recognize the way He chooses to work in our need, but the result will be the same—manna from heaven from a loving God.

Lord, thank You for providing what
Your children need. Amen.

MERCY EMBODIED

*For thou, Lord, art good, and ready to forgive; and
plenteous in mercy unto all them that call upon thee.*
PSALM 86:5 KJV

Mercy is a lofty virtue. Trace the line of world history and you won't find
an abundance of mercy in the stories there. The conquests of explorers
and the defeat of nations usually didn't include mercy for the homeland.
The expansion of human horizons has rarely been accompanied by
peaceful relations.

But follow the history of God's interaction with humankind and you'll
find a story defined by mercy. Start with an ancient Garden and hear
the mercy in the Creator's voice as He promises that someday the Seed
of the woman will crush the serpent. Go on to an oppressed people
making bricks in the Egyptian sun and watch His mercy as He sends
Moses, the deliverer, to lead them out. Continue on to a wayward nation
who embraced the pagan gods of other nations and fell into captivity
and observe Jehovah's mercy as He brings them out again through the
reign of righteous leaders. Stop on a hill outside Jerusalem where an
execution is taking place and experience the mercy as Christ gives His
life to throw wide heaven's gates.

Mercy begins and ends with God. He is the source of it. Apart from
Him, life is bleak and eternity is black. But with Him, mercy abounds—now
and always.

*Lord, thank You for being the
source of all mercy. Amen.*

SUPREME ARCHITECT

For every house is built by someone,
but God is the builder of everything.
HEBREWS 3:4 NIV

Architecture changes with the centuries. Many towns have an historical section where houses from days past can still be seen lining brick streets and towering over the more modern present-day buildings. And every period of history had its hallmark architecture: The Vikings were identified by their ships; castles marked medieval landscapes; the Renaissance had its cathedrals; and the American frontier its cabins.

The philosophies of the generation are displayed in the buildings they created. Whether austere or lavish, big or small—the materials used and the pattern of the rooms tell how people were thinking in that time. It reveals their attitudes toward home and business and their purpose in life.

God is the ultimate architect. What He designs is meant to last. He doesn't create to win the praise of others or to make a name for Himself. His signature is already scrawled across every tiny plant and microscopic organism. His glory is revealed in the magnificence of the sunrise and the pounding of the surf. His creations never go out of style and will last for eternity.

Thank You, God, for the creative genius You
display in everything You make. Amen.

THE HEART HEARER

God is greater than our heart, and knows all things.
1 JOHN 3:20 NKJV

The Bible says that long ago everyone on earth spoke the same language. But one day, at a place called Babel, that all changed. A crew of men was working on a tower, a monument to human achievement—a tower that might even reach up to God and claim His territory too.

God didn't allow that to happen. He knew things they didn't—like how impossible it was for them to reach His dwelling, even if they could overcome the force of gravity and the absence of oxygen and the blackness of space. So to stop their foolish attempt He "confused" the languages. Suddenly, they couldn't understand one another. And the riot that ensued broke up the daring building plan; groups of like-speaking people got together and went away to make new lives.

Now there are numerous languages and dialects spoken among the human family. All over the planet, people voice their prayers to God. And He hears every one of them. But even more amazingly, He hears the heart as well. There in the silent core of each person, God listens, searches, and understands. No matter which language you speak, He interprets every nuance perfectly.

Lord, I'm so glad that You hear my
heart when I talk to You. Amen.

COUNSELOR TO EVERY PERSONALITY

O Lord, You have searched me and known me. You know my sitting down and my rising up; You understand my thought afar off. You comprehend my path and my lying down, and are acquainted with all my ways. For there is not a word on my tongue, but behold, O Lord, You know it altogether.

Psalm 139:1–4 NKJV

Sanguine, choleric, melancholy, phlegmatic—the four temperaments—are descriptions of human personality based on an ancient Egyptian theory later developed by Hippocrates. This theory of the four humors explained that the four basic types of temperament were related to the prominence of one of four fluids in the body. While modern medicine doesn't adopt all of Hippocrates's beliefs, this model is still used today in understanding human personality traits.

Sanguines—the people-oriented extroverts; cholerics—the goal-driven leaders; melancholies—the artistically minded perfectionists; and phlegmatics—the peace-keeping introverts: God made them all. Each reflects His design, and He understands their strengths and weaknesses.

Everyone needs a confidante and counselor, and God has the perfect credentials. The psalmist said that He knows all the little details and is familiar with the inclinations and ways of every personality. Each temperament type has its struggles, and He can offer the assistance. Self-discipline, forbearance with others, humility, and more are available to all who accept Him as Counselor.

*God, help me to discipline myself
and to love others. Amen.*

POMP AND MAJESTY

The LORD reigns, He is clothed with majesty.
PSALM 93:1 NKJV

The human heart craves majesty. It was created in the image of the God who dwells in splendor. Men and women were not created for dirt and thorns and sweat—that was the curse of sin. Humankind was designed to share the glory of God both now and forever.

Man's first home was the Garden, a lush, beautiful place. A place filled with majesty—in the animals, in the vegetation, and in the presence of the Creator who walked with them in the cool of the day.

The future home of humankind is a city, a fabulous kingdom where everything is bathed in light and there is no taint of imperfection anywhere. There is majesty there also—in the angels, the streets, and the great white throne where God rules with love and truth.

The present dwelling of humanity bears only traces of splendor. The faint imprint of past glory is evident in the stretches of white beaches, the dense green of the tropics, and the soaring peaks of the mountain ranges. But someday, those who have put their faith in Christ will actually enter the magnificence of God. With glorified bodies and forever free from temptation and sorrow, they will forever live in glory.

Lord, I praise You for the majesty of Your Being,
and I stand in awe of You. Amen.

HE NEEDS NO DEFENSE

*It is not that he is dilatory about keeping his
own promise as some men seem to think; the fact
is that he is very patient towards you.*

2 PETER 3:9 PHILLIPS

Today's society loves lawsuits. Popular television shows feature civil controversy and "judge" rulings. The Yellow Pages are loaded with advertisements for attorneys wanting to attract clients for everything from injury settlements to divorce proceedings. Big crimes get national news coverage, and the public is fascinated with courtroom drama.

Perhaps some of this arises from a greater emphasis on the law. (Thank goodness, the vigilantes and bounty hunters of the old West aren't in control!) But maybe some of this litigation obsession has come out of the "victim" mentality that destroys so many in our privileged country. Whatever the reason, people today are serious about their own defense.

As believers, we are drawn into this culture of "proof." And, when it comes to the existence and work of God, we want to take up for Him, to defend Him to the skeptical world. They don't accept His grace, they scoff at His promises, and they challenge Him to prove He is real. But He needs no defense. He is not threatened by the naysayers; He isn't harmed by the unbelievers. In fact, He stands by, patiently enduring their anger so He can extend yet another chance for mercy.

*Lord, thank You that Your reputation is one
of mercy even to the doubters. Amen.*

*Affection is responsible
for nine-tenths of whatever
solid and durable happiness
there is in our lives.*

C. S. LEWIS

Praise for

THOSE BELOVED

DELIGHT IN DAUGHTERS

"Many daughters have done well,
but you excel them all."
PROVERBS 31:29 NKJV

When I was expecting my first child, I prayed fervently for a girl. God answered my prayer; not because it was my idea, but because it was His. Whatever reason I might have had for thinking a daughter first would be best, His far exceeded it. I was thinking of satin bows and linen dresses and porcelain dolls, of bouncy curls and piano lessons, and mother/daughter talks after dates. He was thinking of blessing the world through my child—and for the plan He had in mind, a little girl fit perfectly.

As daughters grow, moms realize that there are many causes for delight in them. It goes beyond fashion and fun and fancies of all kinds, though being feminine brings Him glory too. It is thrilling to watch them mature into the fabulous creatures God designed when He formed the first woman in a faraway garden. Her name was Eve, and her momentous assignment was to be the first lady of the new world! Daughters born today won't face a task like that, but still His plan for them will provide plenty of challenges. And moms have the privilege of grooming them for the future.

So take a moment to praise the heavenly Father for the delight of little girls growing up to be women who fit His plan and bring Him glory.

Lord, I praise You that You have a plan for
little girls, and I was one of them. Amen.

A HUSBAND'S STRENGTH

The glory of young men is their strength.
PROVERBS 20:29 NKJV

Put a bunch of guys together at a gathering and the talk soon turns to feats of strength. It might be a discussion about football teams or boxing matches or fast cars or rock climbing. But the odds are great that the topic will involve some aspect of power.

As Proverbs says, this is especially true of younger men. With joy, adolescent boys discover their fledgling biceps and take great pride in showing off their strength. Never before was arm wrestling more serious! Whether it is hitting a ball over the fence or lifting a huge box, the youthful man is ever ready to put his strength to the test while moms chuckle with gentle understanding.

Made for strength—that's the pattern for men. And women who have their wits about them aren't threatened, but ecstatic about it. There is a purpose for everything. The strength of a man's physical and mental powers adds a needed ingredient to marriage and family life. The Creator knew what He was doing when He sculpted those pectorals and biceps and gave males a unique perspective. And every day wives are blessed by husbands whose strength is surrendered to His power—that's the kind of strength that blesses, protects, provides, and cherishes.

Lord, thank You for the strength of men and
the ones who use it to bless others. Amen.

A FRIEND'S UNDERSTANDING

For a friend of mine who is on a journey has just come.
LUKE 11:6 AMPC

Back doors. Cryptic voice mails. Unannounced visits. These are the symbols of true friendship. Acquaintances apologize for unusual words and ways; friends overlook them. That's not to say that friends should be rude or insensitive. Rather, it means that friends can be "real" with each other. They can be real about their emotions, their families, and their shortcomings. False fronts only work on Western movie sets. In friendships, they are barriers.

The friend in Jesus' parable didn't seem worried about his surprise visit or late arrival. He had confidence his friend would welcome him. And the receiving friend set about to do that, even at the price of upsetting his neighbor by asking to borrow some food for a late-night snack. His friend's comfort was important. He'd do whatever was needed to ensure it.

It's a beautiful thing to have a true friend. If she stops by for a visit and there are dishes on your counter or unfolded laundry in the hall, she doesn't bat an eye. If you call her to gripe a little, she'll listen and then tell you to deal with it. If you're late with her birthday gift, she's okay (that means you won't be mad at her when she's late with yours).

Father, I'm grateful for friends I don't
have to pretend with. Amen.

A PASTOR'S CARE

*Obey your spiritual leaders, and do what
they say. Their work is to watch over your souls,
and they are accountable to God.*
HEBREWS 13:17 NLT

A good pastor is a blessing. Just ask the congregation who is without one. Talk to the church who has buried their minister. Spend some time with a church board in the throes of a pastoral search. They'll all agree that a good pastor is valuable.

Of course, the question could be asked, what is a good pastor? The Bible's response is summed up well in this verse, which simply states that a pastor is to "watch over" the souls of those in the congregation.

If you have a pastor who is concerned for your spiritual welfare and shows it by attitude and conduct, you are blessed. But not all pastors are created equal in their manner and approach. Giftedness has many faces, and pastors are as unique as the churches they serve. God is the author of variety; He sends congregations a surprise dish once in a while. And who knows? They may be on the brink of an incredible season.

Pastors are shepherds, and shepherds care. They answer phone calls at three in the morning, spend hours in hospital waiting rooms, attend numerous graduation parties, give counsel, pray prayers, hold babies, field complaints, and share themselves every day of the year—they're worth their weight in gold.

*Heavenly Father, I appreciate my pastor—
the shepherd You've given me. Amen.*

A MOTHER'S CONSTANCY

She watches over the ways of her household.
PROVERBS 31:27 NKJV

Motherhood reflects the heart of God—His devotion and tender care are unending and so are hers.

Motherhood is a demanding job. But little girls start training for it early on. Have you ever watched the way a little girl cares for her baby doll? She dresses it tenderly and then cuddles it against her. She rocks it back and forth with a gentle motion. She takes it with her everywhere; she takes great delight in meeting every need of her little "baby."

Adult mothers are pretty much the same. It usually turns out to be a tougher job than most new mothers expect, but it just comes naturally for women to care for the ones they love, to watch over those in their household.

Who put that nurturing instinct in mothers, real and pretend? God, of course. He had it all planned out that human mothers would reflect His divine heart. That is how they mirror Him.

What a wondrous thing is that kind of love! And women have the privilege of reflecting it to others. Even women without children were designed to care and nurture, and there are numerous opportunities available; the world can never get enough mother-love. How awesome that you and I can be both on the receiving and giving end of that gift!

*God, thank You for the nurturing
love You put in mothers. Amen.*

A COUSIN'S DEVOTION

*"May the LORD watch between you and me
when we are absent one from another."*
GENESIS 31:49 NKJV

We take cousins for granted when we're young, but they're part of the warp and woof of family life. They were preschool playmates and partners in crime. Now they're grown-up confidantes. They grew up with us, watched us mature from awkward adolescents to halfway-decent adults. They carry the other half of the family gene pool. They're the crowd we hang with at family reunions. They show up at our children's weddings and stand solidly with us in our tragedies. Sometimes we live close together; sometimes distance keeps us apart. But the blood tie we share keeps our hearts in rhythm. First, second, third, and even beyond—cousins are an incredible blessing.

Think of two significant cousin relationships in scripture—Mary and Elizabeth, and Jesus and John the Baptist. In a time of vulnerability and confusion for Mary, Elizabeth must have provided strength and understanding. When the Baptizer was facing death and grappling with despondency, he reached out to his cousin, asking for reassurance of His claims. Jesus provided it without condemnation. Cousins show up when they're needed.

If you have a cousin, you're rich. You can't buy that kind of kinship. It's one of those "good and perfect" gifts from God.

*Thank You, Father, for a friend
indeed—a cousin. Amen.*

MANHOOD IN A COCOON

Act like men and be courageous;
grow in strength!
1 CORINTHIANS 16:13 AMPC

If it's true that "men are only boys grown tall," then the little sons around the house are really little men. Before they're born, they bear the traits of manhood.

Watch a little boy with his mother. He wants her affection; he shows it by bringing her dandelions. He wants her admiration; he tries to get it by demonstrating his skill with the ball or bike or trampoline. He delights in the good things she makes for him—warm cookies and special treats. He needs her comfort and nurturing.

It is sweet for a mom to observe this "man in process." When his hands are little-boy rough, when his jeans are grass stained, when his voice is still clear and high, when his young mind is filled with visions of future greatness, a mother can sense in her son that magnetic quality that forms the basis of manliness. He is created for adventure, heroics, and strength. There is an aching beauty in his unfolding. For tomorrow the cocoon will no longer be needed; his day to shine will have come.

God, I praise You for the beauty of little
boys who become heroic men. Amen.

A FATHER'S CORRECTION

For whom the Lord loveth he correcteth;
even as a father the son in whom he delighteth.
PROVERBS 3:12 KJV

Most children don't consider their father's loving correction to be something deserving of praise. But talk to them in adulthood and they've changed their minds.

Little children see only today; fathers see the tomorrows. Kids view their misdeeds as slight misdemeanors; fathers look at the opportunity to keep their children from a "felony" down the road. God has given fathers the ability to see the bigger picture. Listen to a man correct his child. He will talk about why his child must stop the behavior, what it means for the future. This is the heart of God reflected in a good father.

Scripture abounds with references to God as a heavenly Father. He embodies all that earthly fathers are meant to be—strength, love, mercy, faithfulness, support, and much more. Some human men have a difficult time living up to this standard; some don't even try. But wherever a godly man corrects his children in love, there is the image of our God.

Father, I'm grateful for the perfect way in which
You lovingly correct my steps. Amen.

A GRANDPARENT'S INVESTMENT

A good man leaveth an inheritance to his children's children.
PROVERBS 13:22 KJV

A doughnut with sprinkles. Help in sewing doll clothes. An illustration in car mechanics. Fishing trips. Christmas gifts. Birthday greetings. Each of these says "grandparents." From unexpected treats to life lessons, grandparents are all about giving.

Grandchildren are one of life's chief joys. But on the flip side, grandparents are incredibly precious too.

Without grandparents, there would be no need for multiple poses in the portrait sitting, no reason for huge toy aisles in the stores, no excuse for boxes of cookies and Sweet Tarts. If there were no grandparents, most kids would miss a lot of the "unnecessary" things in life—the things parents can't give and grandparents love to.

But good grandparents do more than spoil their grandchildren with unexpected treats. They also are smart investors—they empty their lifelong account of wisdom into young minds. They help a younger generation sort through the litter of life and find the pearls. They leave an inheritance, and not all of it is prefaced with dollar signs.

Thank You, God, for grandparents who take
pictures and leave legacies. Amen.

A TEACHER'S MENTORING

He will guide you into all truth.
JOHN 16:13 KJV

Those who cannot perform well in their field end up teaching—whoever started that rumor should run for cover. Teaching is a tough job, never for the unskilled. In fact, to teach someone else knowledge or skills is often more challenging than simply doing it yourself. It requires another set of skills. A teacher must not only know her subject; she must know how to pass it on.

Jesus wanted to tell His disciples how good it was that the Holy Spirit would come when He left this earth. He wanted them to know just who the Spirit is—His manner, His task. So He likened Him to a teacher. Like a knowledgeable and caring mentor, He leads us into truth. He brings us to the "aha" moments; He helps us understand information and know when to use it.

Most adults can remember a teacher who played a significant role in their development, and teachers are often overworked, underpaid, and underappreciated. But the impact they have on those they instruct cannot be measured. When it comes to the work of the Divine Teacher, the Spirit of God, eternity will reveal the debt we owe.

God, I'm grateful for every good teacher You've
given me, especially Your Holy Spirit. Amen.

O come, behold the works of God,
His mighty doings see;
In dealing with the sons of men,
most wonderful is He.

The Psalter

Praise for
HIS WONDROUS WAYS

SACRIFICE AND INCENSE

Let my prayer be set forth before thee as incense;
and the lifting up of my hands as the evening sacrifice.
PSALM 141:2 KJV

We rarely thank God for prayer. Yet, what would life be without prayer? Without that constant connection to God, without His immediate help in crisis, without the reassurance of His strength, the daily challenge of living would be beyond human means. True, there are those who live without prayer, but they often end in addiction, tragedy, and a hopeless downward spiral.

Prayer is a mysterious thing though. What Christian has not wondered why God desires her to ask Him for something He may already intend to provide? We don't know the answer; all we know is that He wants to be asked, even delights in the asking. Maybe the hidden answer, were it to be discovered, would point to the spiritual development in us as we learn to cast our cares on Him and share the burdens of others.

Prayer is a type of sacrifice offered up to Him. Just as the ancient Hebrews brought both praise and petition to Jehovah with their sacrifices, so we bring both to Him as we lift up our gratefulness and our need. He views the rising of prayer as sweet incense.

Wonderful Father, You gave us the privilege of prayer;
accept my thankful offering today. Amen.

EXTRA DAYS

"The fear of the LORD is the beginning of wisdom, and the knowledge of the Holy One is understanding. For by me your days will be multiplied, and years of life will be added to you."
PROVERBS 9:10–11 NKJV

When Hezekiah, King of Judah, was on his deathbed, God chose to grant him fifteen more years of life. Many of the prayers lifted from hospital rooms today ask for the same. Those who stand in quiet halls whisper petitions that God would extend the lives of those they love.

God is the comptroller of human years. He is the One who keeps the record of the birthdays and death-days. He sees the span of earthly calendars and the stretch of eternity. He knows the time determined in His will. It is in His power to prolong a life if that is in keeping with His purposes.

Medical institutions are filled with those whose days have been extended. Praise is given to physicians, prompt care, improved methods, cutting-edge technology, and advanced drugs. But the One who should top the list is often missing or perhaps referred to vaguely as a "higher power."

Let us be perfectly clear. Whenever life is prolonged, God is at work. Satan wishes only to steal, kill, and destroy. For every hospital bed that is empty because of a patient release, there is another opportunity for praise. He, the Giver and Sustainer of life, is worthy of it all.

Lord, I praise You for the extended time
You've given my family and friends. Amen.

FREE CHOICE

"Choose for yourselves this day whom you will serve."
JOSHUA 24:15 NKJV

God didn't create humans as robots or slaves. He created us with a choice.

The power to choose is fantastic—it means we enjoy a privilege that many don't have. Since the beginning of time, evil has worked to steal the choice of others. The Bible records the fact of slavery and tells of the misery of those held fast in its clutches. Joseph suffered after being wrongfully sold into slavery by his brothers. The Hebrews cried out to God for deliverance from their Egyptian oppressors. Israel and Judah were overtaken by other empires and forced into bondage to them. The early Christian Church was populated with slaves of the Roman Empire.

Think of those whose basic human rights have been stripped away, and then consider the pure pleasure of choice we often enjoy but don't fully appreciate. Every part of the globe has suffered the effects of slavery, and even worse than physical enslavement is bondage of the soul—yet everyone can have freedom from this condition. Every person can choose whom to worship, and whom to follow with her life and energy. God will not encroach upon the rights of each individual to decide for herself. It is your privilege, a power with eternal consequences.

*Thank You, God, for the ability and power
to choose whom I will serve. Amen.*

PRESENCE IN FEAR

*"He is the One who goes before you. He will
be with you, He will not leave you nor forsake
you; do not fear nor be dismayed."*

DEUTERONOMY 31:8 NKJV

It's amazing what the presence of another person can do to alleviate feelings of fear. Even if the other person is a child or someone who can't help in a crisis, there's comfort in knowing you aren't alone.

How much more comforting is the thought that God is present every minute of every day! Not only does He bestow His presence but also He is more than able to supply the strength to meet whatever situation is at hand!

Joshua was tasked with an enormous job—leading two million Hebrew wanderers. This message of God's presence was first given to him. But it was also given to those who would come after him—Gideon, Elijah, David, Esther, and a host of others.

Through the generations, multitudes have discovered that in moments of stark fear, His presence shines greater still. What a cause for praise! The God who calls us and redeems us by His grace is with us in the shadows and frightful valleys. Fear has no power when He is present!

*Heavenly Father, help me to remember that
Your presence outshines all my fear. Amen.*

THINGS THAT ARE KEPT

*Let all the earth fear the LORD: let all the inhabitants
of the world stand in awe of him. For he spake, and it
was done; he commanded, and it stood fast.*

PSALM 33:8–9 KJV

The sovereignty of God is a dreadful, yet wonderful attribute of His character. For mortals, the thought of such power can cause apprehension, even anxiety. Yet those who believe firmly in the holiness of Jehovah can gladly acknowledge and rest in His authority.

To some, sovereignty means control, much like a domineering person who forces his will on others. But God's sovereignty is unlike the orders of a control freak. His power is balanced by His absolute purity and everlasting love. While He has total power over the universe He created, He has also bound Himself by the parameters of His Word. He will not force or coerce; He never manipulates.

In human lives, God's sovereignty is a source of peace. It reassures believers that God's hand is over all the seemingly random details of living. And if He presides over even broken dishwashers and misplaced keys, is He not also the prevailing power over global unrest and natural disasters?

God's sovereignty assures His children that things are "kept." In His hands, the world revolves, births and deaths arrive on time, and those who trust Him need not fear.

*Lord, my heart is filled with praise because
You are sovereign and all-powerful. Amen.*

CARRIER OF BURDENS

"I have made you and I will carry you;
I will sustain you and I will rescue you."
ISAIAH 46:4 NIV

Self-reliance and responsibility have long been prized in Western culture. Americans talk about pulling yourself up "by the bootstraps" and standing on "your own two feet." And admittedly that's much better than slothfulness and whining. Yet, in each life there comes a time when relying on your own strength becomes impossible. At those times, you need help.

The word *carry* implies an added weight. Babies are carried home from the hospital, groceries are carried in from the car, and Bibles are carried to church. Sometimes heavy things are carried—like boxes from the attic; sometimes, only light objects—the daily mail in from the mailbox. But in every instance, the one carrying is picking up something extra to take to another destination.

The heavenly Father will carry His children when He knows they need it. He will not leave them to flounder along on their own. There are times when the feeling of being "borne along" is very real, but often it is only realized in retrospect. Yet He never fails.

What a blessing to know that, when the burdens press hard and human strength is waning, His mighty arms are there to lift us up and over.

Lord, thank You for all the times
You carry me. Amen.

KEEPING SENTIMENT
IN ITS PLACE

*Forgetting those things which are behind, and
reaching forth unto those things which are before.*
PHILIPPIANS 3:13 KJV

Sentiment is sometimes a gift and sometimes a curse. And the ability to appreciate beautiful moments and emotions comes more naturally to some people than others. What some would call sweet others would term sappy. And then there are others who seem almost impervious to sentiment. While their spouses might wish them different, in one way they have an edge over the rest.

God teaches His children this: Yesterday is past—focus on today. The past can either empower or inhibit. If those memories bring to mind the goodness, grace, and power of God, then they are strength even in the remembering. But if they lead to indulgence in fear or disbelief or anger or discontent over the gifts of today, then they become weights that drag the believer further away from His purpose.

The apostle Paul admonishes his readers here never to allow "what is behind" to overshadow "what is before." Humans can't help but feel sadness at good things that are past, but for believers, there is an assurance that better things lie ahead. And that's something to be excited about!

*Father, I'm thankful for the glorious days
ahead for me as I walk with You. Amen.*

HE IS BEFORE AND BEHIND

You have hedged me behind and before,
and laid Your hand upon me.

PSALM 139:5 NKJV

Spend some time around those involved in military service and you might hear them use a phrase like "cover your six." This is just cool slang for "watch your back."

In military operations, who's behind is just as threatening as who's in front. Unlike the code of the old West, guerilla fighters have no regrets about shooting someone in the back—taking out as many as possible in any way possible is the goal. So American fighters work together to cover each other while they advance and "clear" the area. There is always someone covering the "six" position.

The psalmist David was in awe that God knew everything about him—his actions, his thoughts, and his words. And not only that, but God was also both in front and in back of him—he was completely surrounded by this God who created and loved him.

And David is not singled out for this kind of attention; God has a similar dossier on each of His children. No one is more intimately acquainted with you than He. And no one can give you better protection from the assault of Satan than He who is "before and behind" you. No matter which front you are facing, He is present everywhere, all around, for you.

God, it's comforting to know that
You guard me on all sides. Amen.

PUSHING US AND CATCHING US

As an eagle that stirs up her nest, that flutters over her young, He spread abroad His wings and He took them, He bore them on His pinions.
DEUTERONOMY 32:11 AMPC

Baby eaglets are fond of their soft bed. High on a cliff, the nest is warm and secure. But they keep growing and the mother eagle knows the time has come for them to venture out. Unfortunately, the babies aren't too interested in this type of self-improvement. So she pushes the reluctant one out. Up and over the edge he goes, tumbling and clawing at the air. And then with a *whoosh*, Mom is there, catching the youngster on her wings, soaring with him back up to the heights so he can try again. Eventually, he'll learn the drill—when there is no ground, spread your wings and catch the current. But until that time, mom pushes and catches him by turn, always there.

And so God does to us. When we are too comfortable and complacent, He nudges us over the edge, letting us feel the open air but rushing under to catch us until we've learned to glide on our own. Like the mother eagle, His actions are for our good, so that instead of being forever babies, we may venture out into the breadth of His will, experiencing His grace in our lives.

Father, thank You for nudging me over the edge and catching me while I learn to fly. Amen.

*I am beginning to learn that
it is the sweet, simple things of life
which are the real ones after all.*

LAURA INGALLS WILDER

Praise for
SIMPLE DELIGHTS

DINNER OUT!

Go, eat your bread with joy.
ECCLESIASTES 9:7 NKJV

The three sweetest words a man can whisper to his wife are "Let's eat out!" If you're a homemaker, you understand! While women may enjoy planning a menu and preparing delicious meals for the family, a break in the routine is welcome and so special!

Now, rather than the exception, catching meals on the fly has become an ordinary part of the week for many Americans. Though economic downturns may have affected lifestyles to some degree, twenty-first-century families are much more likely to enjoy dinner out than were previous generations. So many times, the delight of the experience isn't fully appreciated.

Sometimes the choice is the casual elegance of a sit-down restaurant; at other times, it's the homey atmosphere of a diner or family steakhouse. Then there are occasions when a fast-food eatery serves up just the right meal for the moment. Whichever destination is chosen, there is delight in it—the lighting, the menu, the *clink* and *chink* of the dishware, the polite murmurs of the waitstaff. And of course, the food! A steaming plate, a frosty glass, a basket of fragrant bread—aah, such extravagance in these simple joys.

God, I'm glad for the experience of dining out.
Help me to enjoy the simple pleasures. Amen.

LUMINESCENCE

*Truly the light is sweet, and it is pleasant
for the eyes to behold the sun.*
ECCLESIASTES 11:7 NKJV

Lamplight in the window, a lighthouse beacon on the cliff, and a flashlight in a storm—truly, as the Bible says, light is sweet. It gives off an aura of hope, comfort, and safety.

Think of how light is part of the memorable events in life. There are glowing candles on a birthday cake, shining tapers in the wedding ceremony, and recessed lights at the funeral home. Crowds enjoy sparkling fireworks at Independence Day celebrations, watch the effects of spotlights in dramatic productions, and are glad for the illumination of floodlights at sporting events.

Some kinds of light are not welcome—flashing blue in the rearview mirror, whirring red on a speeding ambulance, and the sickening orange glow of a house fire. In these instances, light represents trauma, urgency, and loss.

But light catches the attention wherever it appears. It is necessary for life to exist, and it was the first thing God created on the earth. That light was a reflection of the magnificent radiance of His being; it brought energy and strength to the newborn world. It illuminated the splendor of the works of the Creator. It was the very first of His gifts to the future inhabitants of earth.

*Thank You, Lord, for light in
all its forms! Amen.*

THE WORLD OF WORDS

How sweet are thy words unto my taste!
PSALM 119:103 KJV

The printed page is an endangered species. With more and more modes of electronic communication and publishing, book collectors may need less shelf space and more room on their memory sticks. Still, there's something charming about a bound book, the tactile experience of turning a page, the aroma of years of use. It's an experience for the privileged.

In the past, words were preserved on parchments, precious and delicate. Then paper came into use, but before Gutenberg's printing press, few people owned books. The cost and time involved in distributing any kind of written work kept the masses poor in terms of literature. But a German inventor changed all that and suddenly, words were everywhere, for everyone. In Western culture today, most people own many books—some thick, some thin, some intriguing, and some not.

But God's Word is far more than great literature and ancient wisdom. It is the very heart of God in language, living, powerful, and eternal. It is forever true, forever settled. The blessing of those words is beyond measure.

*Oh God, I praise You for Your everlasting Word—
in my hands, in my own language. Amen.*

MAJESTIC STALKS

"For there is hope for a tree, if it is cut down, that it will sprout again, and that its tender shoots will not cease. Though its root may grow old in the earth, and its stump may die in the ground, yet at the scent of water it will bud and bring forth branches like a plant."

JOB 14:7–9 NKJV

There is something visually nourishing about a tree that goes beyond the shade and shelter it provides. The vertical height of a tree pulls the eye up, giving perspective to the view. The living dampness of a green leaf is a reminder that life goes on; the crisp color of autumn foliage proclaims that God creates beauty even in death. Standing tall through one season after another, weathering lightning, blizzards, drought, and age, trees are common symbols of uncommon strength.

God formed these gigantic plants with their rough bark and spreading branches and put some of His majesty in their design. Psalms likens Christians to various trees: palm trees, cedar trees, olive trees—trees that are green, resilient, and flourishing. The Bible says that the Tree of Knowledge of Good and Evil played an important role in the Garden where the first human couple lived. And it promises that another tree, the Tree of Life, will be found in that new place God is preparing for those who love Him. A symbol of majesty, a daily reminder of growth—that's the tree.

*God, I'm thankful for the ordinary tree—
and its extraordinary lessons. Amen.*

CHURCH BUILDINGS

"O Lord our God, all this abundance that we have
prepared to build You a house for Your holy name
is from Your hand, and is all Your own."

1 Chronicles 29:16 nkjv

From massive cathedrals with arched ceilings and marble floors to small-town sanctuaries and country chapels with white steeples—the places Christian believers gather to worship are varied. But wherever the location and design, God's house is a sacred place.

The ancient Hebrews had a tent-tabernacle in which to worship. Because they were a people on the move, they needed a sanctuary that went with them. Later on, Solomon built a lavish temple in Jerusalem. It must have thrilled the Jewish hearts to see the magnificent outline of the temple against the glowing sky; it must have been inspiring to participate in the feast days and sacrifices. What a holy, special place.

It is true that the body of believers is the true "Church"; a building is not actually required for worship. But those who have been without one will testify to the blessing of a sacred spot designated for meeting with God to praise and petition together. There is nothing quite so sweet as a Sunday morning spent in worship—whether in a mountain chapel or a great cathedral. His presence is welcome in both.

Father, thank You for giving us a pattern for worship
and for the places where we can do so. Amen.

GARDENS AND GROWING THINGS

*He turned the desert into pools of water and the
parched ground into flowing springs; there he brought
the hungry to live, and they founded a city where
they could settle. They sowed fields and planted
vineyards that yielded a fruitful harvest.*

PSALM 107:35–37 NIV

Homegrown food is a beautiful thing. Those who garden know the thrill of watching the green sprouts burst through the soil and the hearty pleasure of eating the results of the harvest. Humans have been gardening since the beginning of this earth. The very first couple tended a perfect garden. When disobedience destroyed that perfection, they still tilled the land, but now they were engaged in a battle with the stubborn earth.

Today's gardeners understand that struggle. To bring fresh goodness from the ground requires perseverance and patience. But still, the process of growing things is worthy of praise. Turning the earth, dropping the seeds, and nurturing tiny plants remind the gardener of the work of the Father. Pulling up to a table filled with flavorful garden fare makes her thankful for His provision. He designed the growth process. Veggies aren't pulled from the air or harvested from the waters; humans get to dirty their hands in the rich sod and oversee the cycle of life in its simplest form. Yes, to garden is to know one of the secrets of God.

*Lord, I'm glad for vegetable gardens and for the
lessons learned from tending them. Amen.*

MELODY AND HARMONY

He will make her wilderness like Eden, and her desert like the garden of the LORD; joy and gladness will be found in it, thanksgiving and the voice of melody.
ISAIAH 51:3 NKJV

Little fingers and piano keys are a lovely combination. . .when they're working together. But most mothers have heard many moments of the opposite. Discord is still an unpleasant sound, even when caused by an adorable child. The human ear recognizes and embraces harmony, but recoils from discord.

Perhaps one of the founding concepts of the universe, the dance of melody and harmony plays a role in the orbit of the planets and the rhythm of the seasons. It is a theme that touches almost every part of life. Where there is one, there must be the other. Like salt and pepper, peanut butter and jelly, and sweet and salty, they just belong together.

Harmony has basic rules, and there are even different types of harmony, but one thing is the same, harmony always embellishes the melody in some way. Sure, it's possible to have music with only a melody line, but how ingenious of our God to give even more beauty by creating harmony too! It's up to us to appreciate it and to remind ourselves that it won't be long until those little fingers are making glorious music at the keyboard.

God, thank You for the beautiful combination of melody and harmony. Amen.

PORCH SWINGS

The whole earth is at rest, and is quiet.
ISAIAH 14:7 KJV

Porch swings were made for evening hours. When the sky is dusky pink and turning to soft navy and the crickets are beginning to serenade the world, there's no better place to observe the beauty than a front porch swing. In that quiet hour between the rush of the day and the slumber of the night, nature seems to take a collective breath and relax. It is, for that brief interlude, as if the whole earth is truly at rest.

Most people today don't know a whole lot about real rest. What is generally called rest is a few hours of sleep at night or an afternoon with only a few things on the to-do list. But the rest the body and soul craves is not only an absence of activity, but also a nourishing of the inner self.

Christ asked His earthly followers to get away by themselves and "rest a while"—bodily rest (Mark 6:31 NKJV). And He calls those who would to "come unto me. . .and I will give you rest"—soul rest (Matthew 11:28 KJV).

If there had been porch swings in Bethany, you might have found Jesus sitting on one at the home of Mary, Martha, and Lazarus. Resting Himself, enjoying the company of His good friends, reveling in the beauty of His world, He'd have been right at home, so to speak. And so should we.

Jesus, thank You for setting the example
of what it truly means to rest. Amen.

CLOSER THROUGH COLOR

"Though your sins are like scarlet, they shall be as white as snow; though they are red like crimson, they shall be as wool."
Isaiah 1:18 NKJV

Black-and-white pictures have a definite classic appeal. And part of that appeal is the way the monochromatic tone washes away the stark flaws of true color. If the photos of our ancestors had been captured in color rather than in sepia or black and white, they would not seem as ethereal. Color has a way of closing the distance. A tiger in Africa appears frozen in time in a vintage safari photo; on the color pages of National Geographic, the tiger's presence is real, menacing, and undeniable.

Imagine Hawaii in black and white or a Macy's parade in sepia—doesn't work. God created color to attract the eye and fire the imagination. Little children are drawn to clowns, cupcakes, and candy sprinkles. Polka dots and plaids trigger the brain's happy zone. From birth, humans love color, and God filled our everyday lives with every hue imaginable.

He also uses colors to bring the plan of redemption close to the mind's eye. Remember those little "wordless books"? Black for a sinful heart, red for the blood of Christ, white for cleansing, gold for heaven's splendor, and green for daily growth—these bright hues say that color is the language of salvation.

God, thank You for putting Your message in vibrant color. Amen.

KNEES AND TOES

But God has arranged all the parts in the one body according to his design. . .so that the eye cannot say to the hand, "I don't need you!" nor, again, can the head say to the feet, "I don't need you!"
1 CORINTHIANS 12:19, 21 PHILLIPS

Little children sometimes sing, "Head and shoulders, knees and toes." Kids get a little exercise while singing that old Sunday school tune.

The truth bound up in that little song goes far beyond preschool understanding though. God has designed an intricate body that is codependent in order to fully function. Looking at it from a purely aesthetic point of view, the knees and toes are not the most beautifully appointed parts of the body. The knees are often knobby or bowed and toes come in many odd shapes and sizes, but there would be no walking or running without them. Indeed, these body parts that get the least attention often give the greatest freedoms.

When a toe is broken or a knee must be replaced, then we recognize the worth of these "uncomely" parts. But why wait for a crisis? If your knees and toes are in working order today, you are blessed in no small way.

Creator God, I'm grateful for every detail of Your design. Amen.

The jewels of a Christian are his afflictions. The regalia of the kings that God has made are their troubles, their sorrows, and their griefs. Griefs exalt us, and troubles lift us.

CHARLES SPURGEON

Praise for
INVERTED JOYS

DESERT KNOWLEDGE

*All my springs (my sources of life and joy)
are in you [city of our God].*
PSALM 87:7 AMPC

A desert is a place of want, known more by what it does not have than by what it does. Deserts are known to lack water, shelter, and nourishment. Stories set in the desert are usually about hardship and survival, wandering and suffering.

Sometimes God leads His children through the desert. He alone knows the specific reason, but He intends them for beautification. In the desert, there is a constant sense of thirst, and the spirit is parched for nourishment. Like nomads, we daily trudge through the sand, seeing no end to the vast nothingness—there is no shelter for our dreams, our faith, and our future.

But in this dry, uncomfortable, barren place we discover knowledge that is not found anywhere else. In the desert, we learn that He really can supply what is needed to sustain life. When all the excess is stripped away, His solid love and faithful presence remain. Nowhere is this more clearly seen than in the desert.

The psalmist likens Zion, the city of God, to a place of bounty and complete satisfaction. And when we find Zion, a home for our souls, in Him, we need not fear the desert. For safe in His presence, we'll find that "all our springs" are in Him.

*Father, I praise You for the rare beauty
of Your presence in my desert. Amen.*

A HUSBAND'S OPPOSITENESS

He created them male and female, and blessed them.
GENESIS 5:2 NKJV

Husbands and wives are different. That's an observation that is proven true day after day. They differ not only in physiological, mental, and emotional ways but also in their approach to life. The male perspective for engaging in relationships and solving various challenges is drastically different from the female point of view.

God's Word says He created the distinct and different genders and blessed them. He approved of them. The entrance of sin into the world has warped everything about humankind—including the way the genders relate to each other. What He created as a perfectly matching set is now often like two puzzle pieces that don't seem to fit at all. But the fact remains that His plan included opposites.

The difference of her husband's perspective reminds a woman that he represents the image of God in maleness while she reflects it in femaleness. The Creator chose to pour some of Himself into both, allowing their union to present a complete human image of His glory.

In times of frustration and conflict, the opposing viewpoint of a man can be irritating, but a woman who knows God has a plan will ask Him for grace and look for ways to bridge the gap. After all, his difference is part of the divine image!

Lord, thank You for my husband's oppositeness
that reflects Your design. Amen.

CHANGE

*To everything there is a season. . .a time to gain, and a
time to lose; a time to keep, and a time to throw away.*
ECCLESIASTES 3:1, 6 NKJV

Change is difficult for the human heart to accept. Relationships evolve as one season of life gives way to another, and for mothers, a change in role is a difficult adjustment. As children grow, they slide a bit further away every day, every week, every month. Moms struggle to find their equilibrium.

As daughters, women may resist the changes they see taking place in their own aging parents. The gradual decline in their physical and mental powers and their increasing need for assistance is painful. A small bit of loss is always involved with every birthday, every year passed. And when it comes to friendships, the ebb and flow of life sees to it that there are plenty of adjustments to be made along the way.

Things do not stay the same in this world. Deterioration and gradual death are the results of sin. But, on the other hand, development and maturity is part of God's plan for human beings. Recognizing the difference between the two helps a woman maintain her balance as she navigates a lifetime of transition. And, whatever the changes taking place in a woman's life, the faithful God who does not change will see her through.

*Father, I praise You for Your steadfastness
in every change I encounter. Amen.*

LOST OR TRADED BEAUTY

Beauty is passing, but a woman who
fears the LORD, she shall be praised.
PROVERBS 31:30 NKJV

Read about celebrities who recently gave birth, and you'll not have to look far before you find something said about their "back into shape" routine. Accompanying the glossy pictures of radiant mother and newborn is glowing praise for her once-again tight body and regular exercise regimen.

Unfortunately for most normal women, the money, time, and resources needed to "bounce back" quickly aren't included in the average new-motherhood package. While most moms do make the effort to lose the extra pounds and fit back into their pre-pregnancy clothing, it's not often that a woman comes through the blessing of giving birth without some loss to her body's shape.

Some might call this the "price" of motherhood, but maybe it makes more sense to call it the "trade-off" of motherhood. After all, as Proverbs says so clearly, earthly beauty is a passing thing. Instead of hoarding it up for the few years a woman has before she starts to age, mothers decide to exchange it for a different kind of beauty. The grieving that comes with lost glory can be overshadowed by the magnificent joy of bearing and nurturing a living, breathing little person—a gift from God in heaven. And in that knowledge, a woman can confront the stretch marks and loss of muscle tone with a mix of determination and peace.

Lord, thank You for motherhood and
the unique beauty it brings. Amen.

LIFE AT THE BOTTOM

*Are You not the One who dried up the sea, the waters
of the great deep; that made the depths of the
sea a road for the redeemed to cross over?*

ISAIAH 51:10 NKJV

"At rock bottom," "in the pits," "bottomed out"—these expressions represent that hopeless feeling a person has when she believes that things have gotten as bad as possible. It's a painful, desperate feeling.

Life bottoms out for many reasons—lost jobs, tragic deaths, destroyed relationships, natural disasters, and on and on. Whatever the cause, the bottom is a flat, dark, terrifying place.

The Hebrews knew all about that place. There was no place to hide, no alternate route, and no ship for passage. They were at the end.

But God sustains life everywhere—the bottom is the same as the top to Him. In any angle and from any side, He can extend hope, grace, and rescue. He simply dried up a path right through the water, and instead of lying on the bottom, the Israelites were walking on it. What they feared, the sea, became their means of salvation.

When life bottoms out, there is still hope. We serve a God who can reverse the situation and cause the very pits to become a way out.

*God, thank You that You can reverse the
pits of my life for Your glory. Amen.*

HOW YOU FRAME IT

*I would have lost heart, unless I had believed that I would
see the goodness of the LORD in the land of the living.*
PSALM 27:13 NKJV

Society is crowded with victims—some legitimate and some imagined. All have a reason for their everyday struggles—abuse, genetics, environment. Personal attitude is what separates those who thrive from those who flounder. Often called "getting past" the issue, it means recognizing the wrong, dealing with the fallout, and moving forward.

If the definition of victim is stretched a bit, all of us can claim the title to some degree. Everyone has suffered personal setbacks and raw deals. It might be slander that resulted in damage to one's reputation, or it could be the dishonest dealings of an accountant or investor that resulted in financial loss, or it could even be the decision of a corporation to downsize, causing job loss. None of these outcomes is fair or deserved, yet the bottom line is the same—hardship.

Refusing to be a victim is more than positive self-talk; it's a decision to "frame" all things with the fact of God's goodness. The psalmist said he would have "lost heart" if he had not believed in this absolute truth. No matter the landscape around, the immutable law is this—God is good all the time; He is for us, and nothing can truly defeat us.

*Lord, help me to overcome
through You. Amen.*

THE LEECH OF GUILT

I can do all things through Christ who strengthens me.
PHILIPPIANS 4:13 NKJV

Attaching itself to a living source and draining it of vitality is the lifework of a parasite. These loathsome creatures live off the blood of their hosts. And perhaps no parasite is more repulsive than a slimy leech.

In early America, bloodletting was a common and accepted practice that allowed the "bad blood" to be removed from sick people thereby increasing their chances of improvement. And leeches were one "instruments" used to remove the blood. Thankfully, this practice has fallen out of favor in today's world of medical advances. But there are still many "leeches" present in our lives. For moms, it is the leech of guilt.

Mother-guilt attaches itself to moms of all ages. It lurks unseen, waiting for a vulnerable moment to attack. Not doing enough, not being enough, not having enough, not giving enough. . .all these "enoughs" are actually parasites trying to suck out the very life of a mother. Crushing confidence and draining the many joys of motherhood, mom-guilt is a sadistic enemy.

The apostle Paul was not a mom, but he knew the cure for emotional leeches. Christ's power can destroy the parasites and restore health to damaged emotions. Trusting in His strength, moms can face their jobs with courage and confidence.

*Heavenly Father, I need the enabling
power of Christ to work in me. Amen.*

THE BROKEN POWER OF DEATH

Sin entered the world through one man, and death through sin,
and in this way death came to all people, because all sinned.
ROMANS 5:12 NIV

Human suffering is undeniable. History books, hospitals, and cemeteries testify to its reality. And through the millennia, mankind has struggled to understand why there must be sickness, pain, natural disasters, and war. Instinctively, man knows that there must be a larger purpose than a cycle of hate and destruction.

God sits in the hot seat when people try to find someone to blame for the bad things in this world. And while it is true that God, as Creator and Sustainer, allows suffering, it is not true that He is the cause of it. The scripture tells us that the pattern of death is the result of sin, which first entered our world through the sin of Adam. Since that time, the ongoing effects of death are seen daily on earth—aging, decay, rogue weather cycles, and the violent destruction of life.

Our wrenching hurts are not God's fault, but He is always ready to help us cope with them—to carry us through, to remind us of the promise of heaven where the pattern of death has no power. Jesus holds the keys to hell and death; and because of Him, the assurance of life everlasting is at work in all who believe.

Thank You, Jesus, for being victorious
over the pattern of death. Amen.

CLOSED DOORS

The animals going in were male and female of every living thing,
as God had commanded Noah. Then the LORD shut him in.

GENESIS 7:16 NIV

Christians talk about God "opening doors" for them. This is faith-speak for opportunities He allows to come into our lives. And usually, these God-moments are positive.

Most people enjoy open doors. Children are taught that it is impolite to slam a door in someone's face. A closed door is a clear way to say no.

Sometimes God says no to His children. Trying to follow His leading, believers test the doors that seem to be opening. Certain doors may appear to be the path to greater blessing, but if God shuts it, to yank it open is to disobey His will.

Noah experienced a closed door. The Genesis account says that, after he and his family and all the animals were inside, God closed the door, or as the NIV puts it, God "shut him in." There was no use trying to open that door; it was closed for good. And, in this case, the closed door was for his protection—it was a good thing. Often, the closed doors we face are of the same variety—God has shut us in for our own good. And, while there may be disappointment over the lost opportunity, the future will reveal that greater blessing resulted from leaving the decision up to Him.

Lord, help me to recognize the closed
doors that won't be best for me. Amen.

THE COMPLICATIONS OF THE BODY

*As the human body, which has many parts, is a unity,
and those parts, despite their multiplicity, constitute
one single body, so it is with the body of Christ.*
1 CORINTHIANS 12:12 PHILLIPS

Bodies are wonderful and sometimes frustrating things. When you're young and healthy, with "vim, vigor, and vitality," you hardly pay attention to the workings of your body. It moves when it's supposed to, sleeps well, and responds to the demands made of it.

As you age, you have to learn to work in conjunction with your body, to consider its needs and frailties. And perhaps most frustrating of all are "the golden years," when the body seems to be an enemy, working against your wishes on a daily basis. But, regardless of the pros and cons of the body at any given age, it comes as a whole package, made to work together.

With Christ as the Head, the Church is also made of various limbs, organs, and digits that work together. Like the human body, there are challenges within the unity of the Church. Sometimes it seems that it is working against itself, but it will never truly be paralyzed or unable to move forward. And the parts of the body that seem to be useless serve a purpose that makes perfect sense to the One who created them.

*God, I praise You for the body of believers;
despite our struggles, we are one. Amen.*

*God does not give us everything
we want, but He does fulfill His
promises. . .leading us along the best
and straightest paths to Himself.*
DIETRICH BONHOEFFER

Praise for
SURE AND CERTAIN PROMISES

UNCHANGING EPILOGUE

For we have no permanent city here on earth,
we are looking for one in the world to come.
HEBREWS 13:14 PHILLIPS

The epilogue of a story provides satisfaction. After the plot is resolved, the epilogue gives the details of the days following the story's end. The reader can see how the happenings in the story work together for a joyful future in the lives of the characters.

Even so, the life of every believer has an epilogue. Heaven is known by many names, and each one tells something about the wondrous place it is. The verse here in Hebrews describes heaven as a city—a place to live, a place to settle.

City dwellers on earth have to contend with some negatives—crowds, crime, taxes, and smog. But there won't be any of that in the heavenly city. The radiance of God will be all the light needed (Revelation 22:5) and His presence will be the ultimate joy for eternity.

The promise of heaven is sure; whatever biblical name is used, it will be pure delight and endless peace. Jesus will be there, and all our fears and frailties and sorrows will have passed away. God will make all things new, including human bodies and human understanding. Having this promise to lean on reminds the believer that the epilogue of her life will be a good one—the best is yet to come.

Thank You, Lord, for the sure
promise of heaven. Amen.

ALWAYS THERE

He Himself has said, "I will never leave you nor forsake you."
HEBREWS 13:5 NKJV

There's a certain fear in aloneness. While some people are described as "loners," few truly enjoy being alone all the time. Even the mountain men of the old West had their annual rendezvous when they came together to compete in contests, show off their furs, and swap stories of exploits.

Humans were created by God to need and to desire relationship. Adam was not completely happy without a companion; it wasn't good for man to be alone. So God created Eve, and the gift of earthly relationship was given.

People around the globe find fulfillment in the company of others. Family bonds define the individual and give her a sense of grounding; friendships add depth and meaning to life. But no one can be present at every gathering of friends or family.

God has no such restrictions. He is everywhere, all the time, 24-7. He has promised to be with us always. He is the antidote for our aloneness. He has both the desire to carry out His promise and the power to do so. Wherever we may be, whether plush or pathetic, close to home or far away, He will be right there. There's no geographic location or emotional pit that He cannot fill with His presence. And in that knowledge is security and peace.

*Heavenly Father, when I feel alone I will remember
Your constant presence wherever I am. Amen.*

NO NEED FOR UPDATES

For I am the LORD, I change not.
MALACHI 3:6 KJV

Our culture is consumed with change. Every day brings another model, method, or style. Corporations don't want their products to be forgotten or to become "stale." Designers have no end to their ideas for improvements. The marketing world gleans its lifeblood from an ongoing parade of new things.

Frankly, it's a good thing that there is change on many practical levels. If not for change, twenty-first-century Americans would be driving Model Ts, using telegrams instead of text messaging, and doing without indoor plumbing. Yes, many changes have been good.

But there is one Being who needs no update. Jehovah God never changes and has no need to do so. His character is perfect eternal love and holiness; His ways and judgments are infallible. There is never an occasion when He needs to reinvent Himself or have an overhaul. He even says in this verse—"I do not change."

What a wonderful assurance to know that He is ever the same and that He keeps His word. When the culture around seems so unstable and when the mind cannot keep up with the whirlwind pace of technical advancement, there is comfort in the heart of the believer who worships a never-changing God.

God, thank You for Your consistent, eternal
Being who has no need of change. Amen.

EVERYTHING NEEDED

"Your Father knows that you need these things."
LUKE 12:30 NKJV

Need is a subjective term. People talk about needing this or that—sometimes it's really necessary for life, sometimes not. In fact, many of the things we really do "need" are not required for basic survival.

What are the basics? Food, shelter, and clothing. Having a car is necessary to function in society, but it's not required to keep breathing. So there is a difference between what is needed to maintain human life and what is needed to continue social life.

In times of war and deprivation, human beings discover what is really needed for life. Niceties can be laid aside; even important things can be neglected when compared with real needs like eating another meal or staying out of the cold.

Jesus promised that the Father would supply our survival needs. As He provides food for the birds and covering for the lilies of the field, so He will give us food and clothing and shelter. In His gracious providence, He usually provides much more than that. He cares about utility bills and medical needs and braces for the kids and new tires for the family car. In fact, He already knows we need these things, but He wants us to ask Him, to realize that He can provide them and have the faith to believe He will.

*Father, I'm grateful for Your promise to
provide for my true needs. Amen.*

HOPE—THE LINE OF SECURITY

But I will hope continually, and will
praise You yet more and more.
PSALM 71:14 NKJV

A feeling of despair means that Satan is nearby. To despair is to be without hope, and God is the author of all hope.

Women today need hope, but often struggle with sadness and discouragement. The enemies of hope are many, whether baggage from the past or the uncertainties of the future. Sometimes Satan uses childhood abuse as ammunition for his lies, or it may be family problems that seem to engulf the horizon in bleakness. Whatever the temptations to doubt, we must refuse to give up our handhold on hope.

Like climbers clinging to the secure line that keeps them from falling, you and I must put our confidence in the God who has never failed and who offers hope in any situation. Take your reasons for despair to Him—the family member addicted to substance abuse, that rebellious teenager, those medical bills, the biopsy results—and let Him fan the flame of His loving hope to life in your soul. And you can say with the psalmist, "I will hope continually and praise Him more and more."

God of hope, You are my confidence
and line of security. Amen.

GUIDANCE FOR THE WAY

*Yes, You are my Rock and my Fortress; therefore
for Your name's sake lead me and guide me.*

PSALM 31:3 AMPC

Wouldn't it be nice to have unmistakable leading from God? The Hebrews had such leading. God sent a pillar of cloud by day and a pillar of fire by night to show them exactly which direction to take. And guess what? They were unhappy where He led them. Even the obvious signs of His direct leading didn't make it easier for them to accept the destination.

God has promised to lead His children, and He has done so in many ways and by various means. No other group of people has had the pillar-of-fire type of leading since Moses' days. Yet, no one who seeks the counsel of God goes without an answer.

In the Person of the Holy Spirit, Jesus promised that believers would experience divine guidance. He instructs in all things from the practical to the eternal. He knows where we need to be and works with us so we may find the right path.

Those who don't know Him must try to figure it out on their own, but God's children just have to keep their hearts attentive to His voice and their spirits surrendered to His will. He has promised guidance, and He will deliver.

*Lord, I praise You for the assurance
of Your guidance. Amen.*

FULL AND FREE FORGIVENESS

*But there is forgiveness with You. . .that You
may be reverently feared and worshiped.*
PSALM 130:4 AMPC

Apologies are difficult and unavoidable. As humans, there is no way to escape apologizing for something, even if it's as trifling as bumping into the person ahead in line. For most of us though, we will occasionally need to apologize for more serious offenses.

Apologies are difficult because the feelings of another person are involved. You may not be sure how deeply she was hurt or what her response will be. She may not be willing to forgive when asked.

We can be especially thankful that we don't have to wonder about God's response to our confessions. Not only will He forgive when asked, He offers forgiveness even before He is asked! There cannot be a doubt that this is a promise He will keep. He gave His only Son as the guarantee. Because of Jesus' suffering and death, forgiveness is unquestioningly granted to those who seek it.

A clear conscience is a magnificent thing, and the only way to get it is by claiming the promise of forgiveness. The Father always keeps His word.

*O God, I worship You because You offer full
forgiveness to me through Your Son. Amen.*

SUPER-CONQUERING POWER

For God has not given us a spirit of fear,
but of power and of love and of a sound mind.
2 TIMOTHY 1:7 NKJV

Think of the wars that have rocked civilizations through history and one thing becomes very clear: It's all about power. Men have fought and died for it on a thousand battlefields; empires have gambled on it; kingdoms have fallen in search of it. Dictators have tried to take it from others so they could wield it for their own pleasures and purposes. It was the cause of the coup that sent Lucifer tumbling from heaven to the pit.

God has promised to give believers power—but not the raw, carnal type. The power He gives is held in check by love and a sound mind. Balanced by agape love and the mind of Christ, the power a Christian wields is a threat only to the powers of darkness.

Through Christ's power, a believer can triumph over any obstacle; she can be "more than a conqueror," a super-conqueror. Ask Betty Stam, who transcended death at the hands of Chinese communists; talk to Corrie ten Boom, who overcame the hate of a Nazi camp; consult with Elisabeth Elliot, who defeated tragedy by teaching the natives who speared her husband—these women would tell you that God gives power, Christ-power, that is more than adequate for any task. You and I can rely on His Word and claim the power we need.

Lord, thank You for the power in Christ's name
that helps me be a super-conqueror. Amen.

JOY—THE RADIANT OUTLOOK

May the God of hope fill you with joy and peace in your faith,
that by the power of the Holy Spirit, your whole life
and outlook may be radiant with hope.

ROMANS 15:13 PHILLIPS

Joy can be difficult to define and even more challenging to obtain. Christians talk about the difference between happiness (based on "happenings") and joy (found in Christ). And we want to be joyful; it's a sorry human being who enjoys feeling sad and depressed.

But claiming joy in the midst of the troubles and stresses of life is not an easy thing. Yet Jesus said in John 15 that His joy would remain in us. How can an ordinary woman, wife, mother, grandmother, employee, homemaker find the secret to that joy?

The joy Jesus promised is a radiant outlook grounded in the faith that He is Lord over everything. Following and obeying brings assurance that we're resting in Him; that knowledge brightens the present and confirms the future.

In John 15, Jesus also talked about "abiding" in Him as the true Vine, the source of all spiritual life. As you and I stay connected to Him, His joy is transmitted to us, the branches. This confidence and peace can never be taken from us while we abide in Him. It is settled.

Jesus, I praise You for the joyful outlook
You give me as I abide in You. Amen.

THE SUSTAINABLE EARTH

Your word, LORD, is eternal; it stands firm in the heavens.
Your faithfulness continues through all generations;
you established the earth, and it endures.

PSALM 119:89–90 NIV

There has been a lot of discussion centered on the earth's weather patterns. Meteorologists try to make sense of it and politicians attempt to explain it, but no one really knows the reason for oddly warm winters and absent rainfall. Some Christians say it is God's judgment on the world or even America in particular, and God has spoken through the weather in the past. But there is no firm word that the present weather is God's messenger.

It is possible that the weather has behaved strangely for years and there just aren't the scientific records to prove it. Old-timers have recalled terrible blizzards, droughts, floods, and hordes of locusts. Remember the Dust Bowl of the 1930s? Probably folks then thought the end was near. And yes, the Bible seems to indicate that, in the end times, the weather will be precarious. But God's Word also promises that as long as there is an earth, there will be predictable seasons (Genesis 8:22).

As Noah and his family stumbled out of the ark into the sparkling sunshine, Jehovah God made a covenant and placed a rainbow in the sky as a symbol. The curse of sin has warped nature as well as people, but until God presents the new earth, He will sustain this one.

Thank You, God, for keeping the
earth in Your hands. Amen.

*Earth's crammed with heaven,
and every common bush afire with God.*
ELIZABETH BARRETT BROWNING

Praise for

CREATION'S WONDERS

PRAIRIES OF PRAISE

Let the field be joyful, and all that is in it. Then all the
trees of the woods will rejoice before the LORD.

PSALM 96:12–13 NKJV

Waving grasses on spreading meadows, blue skies that stretch for miles, gophers and mice and prairie dogs scampering here and there—the vignette of the prairie proclaims the glory of God.

Nature is different from humanity: It always points toward its Creator. People turn sour, become prideful, grow bitter, and act rebelliously. But not the world God has made. Even cursed with sin, it still shines with a message that all can hear plainly—there is a masterful God who reigns.

God planted on our globe an unmistakable image of Himself—His creative work. Whether He accomplished it in the original six days of creation or through the means of catastrophic forces afterward, every field and cascade of water, every soaring peak and wooded glen, every shoreline and sunlit valley is His. They praise Him by doing what they were made to do.

Jesus told His disciples that if humankind didn't give God the praise worthy of His name, the rocks themselves would shout out His praises. Everything God made has a voice to glorify Him—the prairies and rocks and mountains are using theirs. Today let the human voices join them in a mighty song of praise.

God, the splendor of Your creation praises You;
I lift my voice along with theirs. Amen.

SHINING TESTIMONY

In them [the heavens] He has set a tabernacle for the sun,
which is like a bridegroom coming out of his chamber,
and rejoices like a strong man to run its race.

PSALM 19:4–5 NKJV

The ancient Egyptians worshipped the sun god, Ra. Greek mythology proclaimed that Helios was the sun deity who drove his fiery chariot across the sky each day. Both the Aztec and Incan empires worshipped the sun, and some Native American tribes still perform an annual sun dance.

Hanging gloriously in the sky, warming the earth, nourishing life, the sun is really a shining testimony to its Creator. The Hebrew word here for *chamber* is *chuppah*—meaning "canopy, covering, a nuptial closet." The brightness of the sun is compared to the countenance of a bridegroom emerging from his honeymoon suite or the radiant power of a well-conditioned athlete eager to run a race.

The glowing sun shouts the magnificent brightness of our God, whose holiness radiates from His being. Moses could not look on the face of God, but saw only His back. When transfigured on earth, Jesus took on a countenance that was gleaming. Revelation says that heaven will not need a sun because the glorious light of God will illuminate the city. For all of these descriptions, the earthly sun is the symbol, the Creator's witness in the sky to a glory we can only imagine.

God, I praise You for the warmth of the earthly
sun and for the glory it represents. Amen.

JAGGED SIGNATURE

"Listen! Listen to the roar of his voice, to the rumbling that comes from his mouth. He unleashes his lightning beneath the whole heaven and sends it to the ends of the earth."

JOB 37:2–3 NIV

Lightning is both awe-inspiring and frightening. The sheer power of electrical force that leaps from it reminds man and beast that it has the ability to destroy. Yet the beauty of its shooting sparks of color holds a fascinating appeal.

Lightning is used to describe the countenance of the angel who rolled away the stone from Jesus' tomb on Resurrection morning (Matthew 28:3). It is also used to illustrate the quickness of Christ's second coming (Luke 17:24) and the violent fall of Satan from heaven after his revolt against God (Luke 10:18).

Clearly, the brilliance and power of lightning are the characteristics God wants us to recognize—the signature traits He wants to display. His bright holiness and limitless power reveal that He is a God like no other. He creates the symbols of His own Being and displays them in nature.

In earthly realms, a signature can be forged by someone who studies it carefully and becomes skilled at mimicking the strokes of the handwriting. But the Creator's signature can never be duplicated. No other can write his name in the heavens like our God.

Jehovah God, I praise You as Master of the heavens and Lord of all creation. Amen.

UNTAMED WINDS

*For behold, He who forms mountains, and creates the wind,
who declares to man what his thought is, and makes the
morning darkness, who treads the high places of the
earth—the LORD God of hosts is His name.*

AMOS 4:13 NKJV

No other natural force is quite like the wind. It has many faces. On a cool spring day, the warming breeze that fans the fresh buds and blooms is a nourishing, hopeful thing. On a hot and humid summer afternoon, a refreshing breath of wind lifts the stagnant air. And on a brisk autumn evening, the swirling winds rustle the fallen leaves and spread the homey scent of wood smoke and baking breads.

But other types of wind can be destructive and deadly. Typhoons bring sweeping combinations of wind and rain that drench the landscape. Hurricanes and tropical storms blow with gale force, battering anything in their paths. Tornados strike unexpectedly, grinding up the countryside obliterating homes, lands, and people.

Natural disasters are often blamed on God. And it is true that He is over everything that occurs on this planet, and in some instances, uses catastrophes to send a message to a rebellious people. But all rogue storms aren't in that category. Instead, they point out that nature has a power that only He could give it, and one day, its rebellious ways will be purged by His coming.

*Lord, thank You for the promise that, one day,
even the winds will acknowledge Your lordship. Amen.*

RAMPANT CREATIVITY

O Lord, how manifold are Your works! In wisdom You have made them all. The earth is full of Your possessions— this great and wide sea, in which are innumerable teeming things, living things both small and great.

PSALM 104:24–25 NKJV

God is a divine genius, not limited by space or imagination or ability. He loves to create, and into His creatures He poured a little of Himself—their compound eyes and nocturnal abilities and homing instincts all declare His glory.

Some of earth's creatures are more beautiful than others. Children delight to pet a kitten, but recoil from an armadillo. And some animals are much more welcoming because there is no danger in their presence. The emotion one has approaching a lamb is quite different from what one would experience in encountering a tiger. Yet, His creativity has no bounds. He crafts humorous eyes on the dragonfly and ungainly necks on the giraffe and awkward legs on the camel and funny striped colors on the monkeys and He calls it good—a fabulous display of His imagination. And in the many "teeming things" on the earth—the beetles, amoebas, scorpions, spiders, and lizards—is even more of His handiwork.

We need eyes to appreciate this rampant divine creativity. The unique and fearsome animals are just as wonderful as the quiet and tame ones. Surely, it pleases the Creator when His brilliant work is recognized and cherished.

God, Your unbridled creativity in creatures great and small fills me with awe. Amen.

FADED BEAUTY;
ETERNAL COLOR

*In my vision I saw a throne had been set up in Heaven,
and there was someone seated upon the throne. His
appearance blazed like diamond and topaz, and all
around the throne shone a halo like an emerald rainbow.*

REVELATION 4:2–3 PHILLIPS

The end of life is often called the "autumn" or the "sunset years." And
if this is a true rendering, then it is a time filled with color and beauty.
Fall is a riot for the senses—the gold and sienna, orange and crimson of
changing leaves cloak the tree line with majestic loveliness; the ripening
pumpkins and gourds give texture and color to harvest fields; the contrast
of black crows on cornstalks and the deep blue of the fall sky complete
a picture of warmth. The sunset is nature's finale as night approaches. In
pink and lavender, turquoise and magenta, the sun sinks into its westerly
bed in a slow farewell.

Both the winter and night are empty of color. Shades of white and
gray dominate the wintry landscape, and night is a black canvas dotted
only by pricks of starlight and the washed-out swatch of the moon's path.
Color is hidden from view.

But eternity will burst with splendor. In that dawning of endless day,
the spectrum of light will be transformed with eternal glory, and the
prisms of heaven will dazzle all who enter.

*God, I praise You for the beauty of every season
and for the color of eternity that awaits. Amen.*

EACH HAS A NAME

He counts the number of the stars;
He calls them all by name.
PSALM 147:4 NKJV

The Big Dipper, Orion, Taurus, Polaris—since the beginning of time, people have been fascinated by the stars. Pagan astrologers used them to predict the future. Runaway slaves used them to guide their flight to freedom. Stranded soldiers used them to point the way to safety. And aviators used them to navigate the night sky.

The ancients gave names to the heavenly bodies, and more have been added in recent years as better technology has allowed the exploration of deeper regions of space. The facts regarding the stars are mind-boggling. Massive spheres of plasma, they are light-years away from earth. The time it takes the light from their burning hydrogen to reach the earth's atmosphere can be measured in tens of thousands of years, which means the twinkling seen in the night sky is very old light. These objects God flung into space are complicated, dazzling, and countless—millions of them, many more than we can see, fill our galaxy.

But He calls them by name. He knows the characteristics of each and the specific name that He gave them. He oversees their brilliant lifespan and watches as they burn and change. They are His lights, and He is acquainted with everything about them.

Heavenly Father, I'm in wonder that You know each
of Your magnificent lights in the heavens. Amen.

NEVER FAR

*If I rise on the wings of the dawn, if I settle on the far
side of the sea, even there your hand will guide me,
your right hand will hold me fast.*

PSALM 139:9–10 NIV

Medieval scholars may have believed the world to be flat rather than spherical. And Columbus's forays into the New World focused attention on unexplored lands. Discovery of the unknown is a powerful drug; those who try it have to have more.

In the days of the American frontier, westward expansion lured adventurous men to travel to unseen vistas. The Klondike and the Yukon were flooded with hordes of fortune seekers willing to take their chances in uninhabited regions. Mount Everest beckons to the climber, the ocean calls to the sailor, and the wilderness draws the explorer.

Sometimes, in a lonely place far from home and loved ones, the adventurer glances heavenward, isolated from all human contact and feeling distant from God. But there is no part of the globe that is far from Him. Every section of earth is His footstool. The barren and the full are alike to Him—He sees the comfortable and the hostile. Wherever a human finds herself, God is ever present and His hand will hold her fast.

*Lord. I praise You for being present in
every region of the earth. Amen.*

BEAUTIFUL LITTER

*"As for the earth, from it comes bread, but underneath
it is turned up as by fire; its stones are the source
of sapphires, and it contains gold dust."*

JOB 28:5–6 NKJV

If the earth's wonders are God's handiwork, then the remnants of His masterpiece also have glory. A craftsman usually leaves behind traces of his work. Underneath the woodworker's bench are shavings and bits of carving; beside the potter's wheel are pieces of clay with half-finished designs; on the artist's palette are swaths of mixed color; and in the seamstress's basket are scraps of fabric with tiny seams. Each item that is leftover from the master's labors is a testament to the skill brought to the task and the design behind it.

Unwanted bits of paper and plastic strewn on the roadways and sidewalks are called litter. But the litter God leaves isn't really litter at all; it is a witness to glory. Think about the shells scattered on the beach—discarded homes of sea-dwelling creatures; and the pebbles lining the lakeshore—bits of shale and crystal, small and insignificant. Acorns dot the forest bed and pinecones lay among the pine needles, unheeded by most passersby. These are God's disposables, beautiful even in their unwanted state. Perhaps there's a reason why children delight in collecting rocks, shells, pinecones, and acorns; maybe they can better see the glory that infuses each little thing.

*Father, thank You for giving glory to the
disposable things in Your world. Amen.*

LIQUID OF LIFE

You care for the land and water it; you enrich it abundantly.
The streams of God are filled with water to provide the
people with grain, for so you have ordained it.

PSALM 65:9 NIV

Water is the source of continuing life. Neither man nor beast can survive long without it. Some even believe that water was the beginning of life; they conclude that the very first form of life began in primordial waters and evolved over time into the life forms known today.

Those who know the truth of God's Word reject this theory of origins, but do affirm that water has a connection with life on earth. Genesis 1:2 says that the earth in its beginning stages was covered with water, and from this darkened womb, God crafted all things, living and breathing.

Obviously, God intended that there would be a link between water and life. And it is His ongoing provision of water that keeps life going on the earth. The astronauts say that, from space, the earth is defined by the presence of water. It is referred to as the "blue planet." Set apart from the other heavenly spheres by this life-giving liquid, the earth is special. It was intended to nurture God's creatures.

Water is very common, yet extremely important. And the God of heaven supplies it every day.

Father in heaven, thank You for
life-giving water. Amen.

Grace and glory differ very little;
the one is the seed,
the other is the flower;
grace is glory militant,
glory is grace triumphant.
THOMAS BROOKS

Praise for

WHISPERS OF GRACE

THE LITTLE CLICKS

"When He, the Spirit of truth, has come,
He will guide you into all truth."
JOHN 16:13 NKJV

Morse code is a language all its own. Made up of clicks of varying lengths and types, it is instantly recognizable to one who knows its secret. Developed through the efforts of several men and refined through the years, this code has been effectively used for over 150 years.

The Holy Spirit speaks in a language of the soul. Jesus promised that He would guide believers into all truth, and when a person receives Christ as Savior, the Spirit becomes an ever-present Companion and Teacher. He illuminates scripture for our understanding and brings to mind needed principles at just the right moment. And He keeps the heart accountable.

The "clicks" of the Spirit are those little pricks of conscience we feel when we're tempted to make a hasty decision or say something that wouldn't bring glory to God or behave in a manner unpleasing to Christ. Like the clicks on a telegraph wire, those quiet, holy reminders from the Spirit are God's way of communicating with our souls.

God cares about His children, and He wants to help them stay close to Him. The nudges and reminders from the Holy Spirit are the emergency language of heaven—by listening to it, believers can avoid disaster.

God, I'm so grateful for the clicks on heaven's
wire that keep me out of trouble. Amen.

LUXURIOUS CLEANSING

*"For He is like a refiner's fire and
like launderers' soap."*
Malachi 3:2 NKJV

Soap and water are luxuries. After jogging or gardening or cleaning out the attic, nothing is more refreshing than a shower.

In the past, when water had to be conserved as drinking water for livestock and people, bathing was a treat and not taken for granted like it is today. Women had to face the challenges of home and family life without the benefit of running water. And in some third world countries, it is still much the same. So the blessing of a nice bubble bath is one to be appreciated.

But the benefit of spiritual cleansing is of much greater importance. The cleansing Christ offers is more than surface cleaning; it is a scouring of the soul and spirit. With the fire of His holiness and the purity of His nature, He refines the surrendered heart and removes the impurities of sinful motives and selfish desires. Those who pass through the cleansing He offers are renewed, refreshed, and blessed.

*Lord, thank You for the deep cleansing
You offer the soul who desires it. Amen.*

MATURATION IS A PROCESS

*But let patience have its perfect work, that you
may be perfect and complete, lacking nothing.*
JAMES 1:4 NKJV

Growing up is something all little girls want to do. Somehow the seed of womanhood locked into those tiny hearts longs to spring up and mature. Baby dolls awaken the longing for motherhood. Tea sets and dress-up clothes nourish the sentiment for gentle and lovely femininity.

But it takes years for adulthood to arrive. There are a lot of things to experience before having a home to care for, babies to tend, and a grown-up life. There must be science experiments and English papers and braces and bad hair days and Driver's Ed and Home Economics and college exams and lots of hard work. The girls who try to rush the future are the ones who end up enjoying it the least.

Growing into anything requires patience. God knows that we're not going to be mature in our faith after only a short while. He wants us to understand that, like little girls have to grow up a day at a time, so we must grow into maturation and completion one obedient step at a time.

His grace provides all that is needed at every level, and His promises keep the future secure. We will get there if we let patience have her perfect work in us.

*Father, I praise You for helping me grow
in You at just the right pace. Amen.*

HE GIVES REPEAT LESSONS

Trust in the LORD with all your heart,
and lean not on your own understanding.
PROVERBS 3:5 NKJV

Some things are learned in one easy lesson; others take more time. Touching a hot stove once is usually enough to learn that heat can burn. But learning that money should be saved and not spent immediately is a lesson that might require longer.

When it comes to a person's relationship with God, lessons are always being learned. The classroom of grace is never closed. It stays open 365 days a year. And that's a good thing.

The Holy Spirit is a gracious teacher. He's looking for surrendered hearts and obedient spirits. He sees the effort put forth and the progress being made. And He is patient when some lessons have to be repeated.

Trust is one of those issues. Perhaps it's because humans have difficulty getting beyond the need to see and touch; maybe it's because Satan works so hard to cause us to doubt. Whatever the reason, learning to trust God's ways in our lives usually requires extra time. But the quicker the learning, the sooner the benefits are experienced. And the honor roll of heaven means peace and security for the student.

God, teach me to trust You,
and let me be a good student. Amen.

SEALED AND KNOWN

*But God's truth stands firm like a foundation stone with
this inscription: "The LORD knows those who are his."*
2 TIMOTHY 2:19 NLT

Identification is very important in today's world. Actually, it has always been. In biblical times, being able to prove what tribe you were from was key. In fact, the famous "begat" passages of scripture were vital to those who were keeping track of family lineage within Israel. During the New Testament period, identification as a Roman citizen had distinct advantages; the apostle Paul was able to appeal to the higher courts of the land and even to Caesar because of his citizenship.

Identification has been linked to aristocracy, privilege, and even personal freedom in regimes like Nazism and Communism. Today, identification is something to be protected with identity theft on the rise and social media in constant use. And the Bible seems to indicate that future times will bring even more emphasis on one's identification.

The personal identification of God's child is safe. God knows those who belong to Him; they bear His seal. He can't lose them amidst the shuffle of the world's billions. Each of them is distinctly visible to His sight, at all times, in any place.

*Lord, thank You for marking me with Your
name and knowing who I am. Amen.*

THE SIGNIFICANCE OF PLACE

*Like a bird that wanders from its nest is
a man who wanders from his place.*
PROVERBS 27:8 NKJV

Psychologists tell us that our environment is important. For babies to develop properly, they need a loving setting. Children must have love and encouragement to grow into healthy adults—and to function at their best as grown-ups.

People have a need to know where they belong and how they fit in. Like the nest centers the wandering bird, so a home centers a person. Wherever she goes during the day, whatever hostilities and stresses she may face, at the end of the day there is a place of welcome and retreat.

But beyond a physical home, people also need to know their spiritual place. God has provided for each believer a sphere of ministry and fellowship that will fulfill her and keep her grounded. But often we are tempted to look beyond the perimeters of our setting and yearn for what others have. They seem free to indulge in things we cannot; they appear more blessed. But the place God assigns is the best and to wander from it is to invite discouragement and ultimately, defeat.

Those who disdain the place that God has ordained for them will forever fight feelings of discontent. But for the woman who embraces her physical and spiritual home, there is balance, peace, and focus.

*Father, help me to always have both peace and
contentment in the home You have given me. Amen.*

RELATIONSHIP IS
WHAT MATTERS

*Being confident of this very thing, that He who
has begun a good work in you will complete it.*
PHILIPPIANS 1:6 NKJV

Women often measure their lives by events and dates—first date, first kiss, first formal gown, wedding day, babies' births, and anniversaries. More so than men, women mark time by the significant relationships in their lives.

When it comes to relationship with God, it is easy to start measuring it in the same way. Especially for conscientious souls who are driven to keep track of their progress and chart their successes, the orderly march of events is important. Listening to an older believer talk about her Christian journey causes introspection and sometimes discouragement. Often, it seems there isn't a perfect record on the progress report. In fact, it may seem that the present isn't as good as days before.

For anyone who wishes to obsess with mile markers, the apostle Paul wrote these words: "You may be confident that He who started this good work in you will complete it"—the record is about your relationship. Staying connected to Him results in progress, and one day, the final report will prove it. Dates and events and statistics are wonderful, but what matters most is not what you did yesterday, but how your relationship with Him is today.

*Lord, I praise You for the work You're doing in me
and for the completion date ahead. Amen.*

MENDED PEOPLE

*My brothers, if any of you should wander away from the truth
and another should turn him back on to the right path, then
the latter may be sure that in turning a man back from his
wandering course he has rescued a soul from death, and his
loving action will "cover a multitude of sins."*
JAMES 5:19–20 PHILLIPS

It is difficult for people to forgive the failings of others and go on to form
relationships that rise above them. The human spirit wants to remember
the events of the past and base future actions on them. But when a
restoration has taken place, it is time to close the gap and allow the shifted
sand to fall back into place.

The problem is that most of us reject mended things; we prefer items
that don't have repair lines. It seems much better to have something whole
in the first place than to have an object that was obviously restored from
a battered condition. And in dealing with cars and homes and pianos and
computers, that's probably true. But with people, "mended" means that
the Divine Restorer has been at work. And that indicates that the person
is better because the state of anyone "before" Christ isn't good or whole.

When a person comes back to Christ for redemption and healing, it is
the privilege of the body of believers to assure her that the past is forgiven.

*God, thank You for mending people,
including me. Amen.*

ADOPTIVE LOVE

He planned, in his purpose of love, that we should be adopted
as his own children through Jesus Christ—that we might learn
to praise that glorious generosity of his which has made us
welcome in the everlasting love he bears towards the Son.
EPHESIANS 1:5–6 PHILLIPS

There is no love quite like adoptive love. It reaches out to make another
belong, to offer a part in the family home and in the family legacy.

God's Word uses the word *adoption* to describe the way God brings
children into His family. Jesus, the only begotten Son, was willing to die
so that brothers and sisters might be added to the heavenly family. God,
the Father, was willing to share His glory and His home with those who
weren't looking for Him.

Adoption proceedings require ample proof that the parents can
provide for the child they wish to adopt. If they cannot meet the standard,
they cannot have the child. This verse in Ephesians shows His glorious
generosity and His everlasting love. No other being on heaven or earth
could offer the lavish provisions that He does.

Once they're part of a family, the days of abandonment are over;
the adopted child belongs. And so it is with God's family. Joint heirs with
Christ and a child of the King—that's what being adopted by God means.

Father, I'm glad to belong in
Your family. Amen.

CORRECTION MEANS LOVE

My son, do not despise the LORD's discipline,
and do not resent his rebuke.
PROVERBS 3:11 NIV

Few people enjoy correction. To be told you've done something wrong isn't pleasant. It's humiliating and irritating, and most people try either to avoid doing something wrong or to avoid being caught while doing it.

Yet, the prisons are filled with those who have been caught "red-handed." Some are repentant and actually make an attempt to mend their ways; some are simply furious at the ones who told them they were wrong. For the angry souls, the journey of life will not grow easier, but harder.

Everyone, at some point in her life, must be corrected. It's the way things are. No one "does" life without error, though fortunately, the mistakes don't have to be of the illegal variety.

And in living the Christian life, there will be times of rebuke and discipline. Just as no earthly child grows up without correction, no child of heaven does either. But God's discipline is not to be disdained or rejected, but rather it should be embraced. Discovering where one has erred gives wisdom so the same mistake will not be repeated. Accepting correction with an open heart shows strength, not weakness. And the humility gained is another step to the heights.

Father, I know You correct me when I need it;
help me be quick to listen. Amen.

Every happening, great and small,
is a parable whereby God speaks to us,
and the art of life is to get the message.

Malcolm Muggeridge

Praise for
RANDOM BENEFITS

ICE CREAM

*And people should eat and drink and enjoy the fruits
of their labor, for these are gifts from God.*
ECCLESIASTES 3:13 NLT

The American populace eats enough ice cream annually to fill the Grand Canyon. Now that's a lot of cones and sundaes and pie à la mode! But then, ice cream is known as the "Great American Dessert." However, long before Nancy Johnson of Philadelphia patented her crank ice-cream freezer in 1843, people around the world were experimenting with ways to make this delicious frozen treat. The Persians, Romans, Arabs, and Chinese are all said to have played a part in the early development of ice cream.

Today, modern refrigeration and mass production make the ice cream industry big business. There is almost any imaginable variety, both of texture and of flavor. Low-fat or premium, sorbet or custard, ice cream caresses the palate and pleases the taste buds.

It also reminds us of the greatness of God. He created the cows, which give milk to make the cream, and He provides the sugar cane in the fields. He has allowed man to discover the secret of electricity and the workings of refrigeration needed for the machinery. He instilled in nature the freezing properties and designed the molecules of air that contribute to the texture. He gave humans searching minds and the will to create something new. And with every dish of ice cream served, His greatness shines through.

*Lord, thank You for the pleasure of
eating ice cream. Amen.*

GOING TO THE CITY

Then I, John, saw the holy city, New Jerusalem,
coming down out of heaven from God,
prepared as a bride adorned for her husband.
REVELATION 21:2 NKJV

Cities mean people, many people. The first mention of a city in the Bible is the one built by Cain in Genesis 4:17. And his descendants were noted as skillful men of husbandry and craftsmanship. Cities have also been associated with great wickedness, as the "cities of the plain" (Genesis 13:12) and the cities of Nineveh and Babylon. And it seems likely that the place where the prodigal son wasted his inheritance was a city. Throughout history, rural villages have been associated with decency and morality and cities have been seen as cesspools of sin.

On the other hand, Jerusalem is referred to as "Zion, the holy city" by scripture, and the New Jerusalem is a city with twelve gates and streets of gold.

There are many great cities in our world—New York City, London, Paris, Tokyo, Singapore, Rome, and Hong Kong. Each of them has beautiful landmarks, and all of them share in crime, corruption, and misery. But their gleaming towers and soaring church spires and sprawling residential sections remind the believer that strolling down a city boulevard is just a little taste of the grandeur of heaven, whose glory awaits.

God, thank You for earthly cities and for
the heavenly one still to come. Amen.

PATTERNS, PUZZLES, AND PROVIDENCE

*Moreover we know that to those who love God,
who are called according to his plan, everything
that happens fits into a pattern for good.*
ROMANS 8:28 PHILLIPS

There are seasons of life when nothing seems to jibe. The edges of the week are always off, the angles of family relationships never meet, and the lines of daily life and purposeful living do not intersect.

And then there are those rare, amazing, unexpected times when every event seems to fall effortlessly into place. It's like a perfect matching of round pegs and round holes or the flawless fit of puzzle pieces—a beautiful thing.

At such times, it's good to stop and acknowledge the activity of the heavenly Father who orchestrates the score of our lives for our good and His glory. Scripture promises that His plan will be accomplished and that every nuance fits into the pattern He has designed. And on those days when we get a brief glimpse of the finished work of art, a woman's heart can rejoice in the providence that is always active in the lives of believers.

Irritating days will come again; weeks that seem off-kilter come and go. But resting in the knowledge of His sovereign plan means it won't always be that way.

*Father, I praise You for Your providence
at work in my life and family. Amen.*

THE GIFT OF TEXTURE

*Take from among you an offering to the Lord. Whoever is of
a willing and generous heart, let him bring the Lord's offering:
gold, silver, and bronze; blue, purple, and scarlet [stuff],
fine linen; goats' hair; and rams' skins tanned red, and skins
of dolphins or porpoises; and acacia wood.*
EXODUS 35:5–7 AMPC

Texture can go unnoticed by those who aren't artists. But talk to sculptors, clothing designers, painters, chefs, and interior decorators, and they'll tell you just how important texture is.

God could have made all the surfaces on earth smooth. He could have given humans a coarse hide like some animals. He could have made tree trunks and blades of grass and flower petals feel identical. But He didn't. He gave the gift of texture.

Not only did He create the texture of pinecones and moss and sand, but He also gave humans the perfect organ with which to appreciate His gift—skin. The receptors in our skin are wondrous things, letting a woman appreciate everything from the downy head of her newborn to the moist freshness of garden soil.

Even in the worship offerings presented to Him, God allowed variety of type and texture. These items were to be used to beautify His tabernacle, and He encouraged variety. The world without texture would be bland; instead, God created a playground of sensory delight.

*Thank You, Lord, for the diverse textures in
the world You've given me to enjoy. Amen.*

ENCOURAGING AND PRACTICAL JOURNALS FOR YOUR QUIET TIME

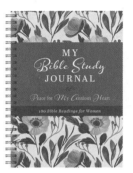

My Bible Study Journal: Peace for My Anxious Heart

This great journal features Bible reading plans that will encourage you to experience more fully the peace of Jesus, as you learn to trust Him. It's perfect for your own personal quiet time or small group study!

Spiral Bound / 978-1-64352-862-5 / $9.99

Discovering God in Everyday Moments Devotional Journal

Here is a delightful devotional journal that celebrates the presence of the heavenly Father in life's everyday moments. 180 thought-provoking readings will speak to your heart, sharing spiritual truths from God's Word.

Spiral Bound / 978-1-64352-729-1 / $9.99

Find These and More from Barbour
Books at Your Favorite Bookstore
www.barbourbooks.com

BARBOUR
PUBLISHING